United States Presidents

James K. Polk

Anne Welsbacher
ABDO Publishing Company

visit us at
www.abdopub.com

Published by ABDO Publishing Company 4940 Viking Drive, Edina, Minnesota 55435.
Copyright © 2001 by Abdo Consulting Group, Inc. International copyrights reserved in
all countries. No part of this book may be reproduced in any form without written
permission from the publisher.

Printed in the United States.

Photo credits: Corbis, Stew Thornley

Contributing editors: Tamara L. Britton and Christine Phillips
Book design and graphics: Patrick Laurel

Library of Congress Cataloging-in-Publication Data

Welsbacher, Anne, 1955-
    James K. Polk / Anne Welsbacher.
        p.   cm. -- (United States presidents)
    Includes index.
    Summary: A biography of the eleventh American president, whose term in office
saw many western states added to the United States.
    ISBN 1-57765-246-0
    1. Polk, James K. (James Knox), 1795-1849--Juvenile literature. 2. Presidents--
United States--Biography--Juvenile literature. [1. Polk, James K. (James Knox), 1795-
1849. 2. Presidents.] I. Title. II. Series: United States presidents (Edina, Minn.)
    E417.W45   1999
    973.6'1'092--dc21
    [B]   98-24017
                                                     CIP
                                                     AC

Contents

James K. Polk

*J*ames K. Polk was the eleventh president of the United States. He helped the U.S. gain more than 500,000 square miles (1.3 million sq km) of land. He also improved the U.S. economy.

Polk grew up on a farm in Tennessee. He did not go to school until he was 17 years old. But he was a good student. He graduated from college and became a **lawyer**.

Polk married Sarah Childress. They did not have any children.

Polk served in the Tennessee and the U.S. **Houses of Representatives**. Then he was governor of Tennessee. In 1844, he was elected president. His election surprised many people.

While he was president, Polk led the U.S. in a war against Mexico. He established the border between Oregon and Canada. During Polk's presidency, the U.S. **expanded** from coast to coast.

President James K. Polk

James K. Polk (1795-1849)
Eleventh President

BORN:	November 2, 1795
PLACE OF BIRTH:	Mecklenburg County, North Carolina
ANCESTRY:	Scots-Irish
FATHER:	Samuel Polk (1772-1827)
MOTHER:	Jane Knox Polk (1776-1852)
WIFE:	Sarah Childress (1803-1891)
CHILDREN:	None
EDUCATION:	Private schools, University of North Carolina
RELIGION:	Presbyterian
OCCUPATION:	Lawyer
MILITARY SERVICE:	None
POLITICAL PARTY:	Democrat

OFFICES HELD: Tennessee House of Representatives,
                                 U.S. House of Representatives,
                                 Speaker of the House, governor of
                                 Tennessee
AGE AT INAUGURATION: 49
YEARS SERVED: 1845-1849
VICE PRESIDENT: George M. Dallas
DIED: June 15, 1849, Nashville, Tennessee, age 53
CAUSE OF DEATH: Chronic diarrhea

Detail
Area

NORTH CAROLINA
Mecklenburg
• County

Birthplace of James K. Polk

Early Life

*J*ames Knox Polk was born on November 2, 1795, in Mecklenburg County, North Carolina. His parents, Samuel and Jane, farmed the land. James was the oldest of ten children.

When James was 11, his family moved to Columbia, Tennessee. They cleared the land to start a new farm.

James was small for his age. He was often sick. He could not help on the farm. And he could not go to school. So he was **tutored** at home.

When James was 16, a famous doctor named Ephraim McDowell operated on him. The doctor removed stones from James's **urethra**. Afterward, James felt much better.

In 1813, James went to a nearby school. He loved school and studied hard.

James became stronger and healthier. In 1814, he went to the Bradley Academy in Murfreesboro. There the lessons were more challenging. And he met many new people. He became friends with Anderson Childress and his sisters, Sarah and Susan.

At Bradley Academy, James studied Greek, Latin, math, and reading. He also acted in school plays.

In 1815, James entered the University of North Carolina. He was one of the university's best students. He was also skilled in **debate**. In 1818, James graduated at the top of his class.

After graduation, James got sick again. He had to stay in North Carolina until he was better. When he reached home in the fall, James decided he wanted to be a **lawyer**.

The University of North Carolina

Polk in Politics

Polk went to work for Felix Grundy in Nashville, Tennessee. Grundy had been a state supreme court judge and a member of **Congress**. Grundy helped Polk study law.

Felix Grundy

In 1819, Grundy also helped Polk become a clerk in Tennessee's state **senate**. Polk kept studying to be a **lawyer**. In 1820, he passed the **bar exam**. He returned to Columbia and opened his own law firm.

At a party, Polk noticed a pretty, young woman with brown hair. It was Sarah Childress. She was grown up now. She had gone to college and studied many of the subjects that Polk did. He and Sarah began to date.

10

In 1823, Polk made two big decisions. He decided to run for the Tennessee **House of Representatives**. He won the election. Then he decided to ask Sarah to marry him. They were married on New Year's Day, 1824.

In the Tennessee House of Representatives, Polk voted against a law to use federal money to build roads and canals in the states. He thought taking money from the federal government would take away each state's independence.

Sarah Childress Polk

Polk also supported General Andrew Jackson for president in 1824. But Jackson lost the election.

Later that year, Polk decided to run for the U.S. House of Representatives. In 1825, he won the election. Soon, he left Tennessee for the U.S. capital.

Representative Polk

*P*olk was elected to the U.S. **House of Representatives** seven times. He was honest and worked hard.

In the House, Polk proposed to sell federal lands in each state to finance education. Polk also proposed that the people elect the president and vice president directly, not through the **electoral college**. But these laws did not pass.

Polk voted against a bill to improve U.S. roads and canals. He thought it was a poor use of the country's money. He also voted against building a road across Panama. He thought the money should be used to improve the U.S. These laws did not pass, either.

In 1832, Polk was elected chairman of the **Committee** on Ways and Means. He urged an **investigation** of the United States Bank. Polk thought it was dangerous for one bank to hold all the nation's money. The bank closed in 1836.

In 1835, Polk became **Speaker of the House**. He tried to keep order during **debates** on slavery. He thought **Congress** had no authority to act on slavery. This made many people mad at Polk.

Later that year, Polk voted against the Distribution Act. This act divided the nation's **surplus** money between the states. Polk thought it would be better to lower taxes and avoid future surpluses. But the act passed anyway.

In 1839, Polk was elected governor of Tennessee. He **eliminated** more than one million dollars in **debt**. He limited the amount of paper money banks could print. He also created a new **committee**. It decided the best ways to improve the state before any money was spent.

Polk ran for governor two more times, in 1841 and 1843. But he was not elected. Some people thought he was working for the rich, not the common people.

In 1844, Polk wanted to return to national **politics**. He hoped the **Democrats** would name him their candidate for vice president at their **convention** in Nashville, Tennessee.

The U.S. Capitol Building in 1827

The Making of the Eleventh United States President

1795
Born November 2 in Mecklenburg County, North Carolina

1806
Family moves to Columbia, Tennessee

1814
Attends Bradley Academy

1815
Attends University of North Carolina

1820
Passes bar exam; opens law firm in Columbia

1823
Elected to Tennessee House of Representatives

1824
Marries Sarah Childress

1825
Elected to U.S. House of Representatives

1839
Elected governor of Tennessee

1841
Loses election for governor of Tennessee

1843
Again loses election for governor of Tennessee

1844
Elected president of the United States; U.S. annexes Texas

James K. Polk

". . . binding together in the bonds of peace and union this great and increasing family of free and independent states, will be the chart by which I shall be directed."

1818
Graduates from university; studies law under Felix Grundy

1819
Elected clerk in Tennessee state senate

1832
Becomes chairman of Committee on Ways and Means

1835
Elected Speaker of the House

Historic Events
during Polk's Presidency

★ Johann Galle and Louis d'Arrest discover the planet Neptune

★ Elizabeth Blackwell is the first woman to earn a medical degree

★ Smithsonian Institution established

1845
Sends John Slidell to make peace with Mexico

1846
Independent Treasury Act signed; Mexican War begins; Oregon Treaty signed

1848
Mexican War ends; Treaty of Guadalupe Hidalgo signed

1849
Returns to Tennessee; dies June 15

PRESIDENTIAL YEARS

Dark Horse Election

*D*uring the 1840s, the **Democrats** argued about Texas. They discussed if it should be a state and if it should have slavery. They also **debated** about where the Oregon Territory's northern border should be.

In 1844, these arguments split the party into small groups. At the Democratic **convention**, each group produced a candidate for president.

The Democrats voted seven times. But no candidate got enough votes to be **nominated**. Then they decided to make Polk a candidate.

On the eighth vote, Polk was third behind Martin Van Buren and Lewis Cass. But on the ninth vote, representatives of every state cast all their votes for Polk. This **united** the party behind one candidate.

Martin Van Buren

16

In the 1844 election, **Whig** candidate Henry Clay ran against Polk. Clay served in the U.S. **House of Representatives** and **Senate**. He was **secretary of state** under President John Quincy Adams. He was a tough **opponent**.

Andrew Jackson campaigned for Polk. Polk was clear about his opinions. He wanted to **annex** Texas. He also wanted to claim the Oregon Territory just north of the fifty-fourth **parallel**. Many people agreed with Polk. "Fifty-four Forty or Fight" became his campaign **slogan**.

Polk won the election. He was younger than any president before him. He was also the first president whose election was a surprise. He was called the **dark horse** candidate.

Henry Clay

The Seven "Hats" of the U.S. President

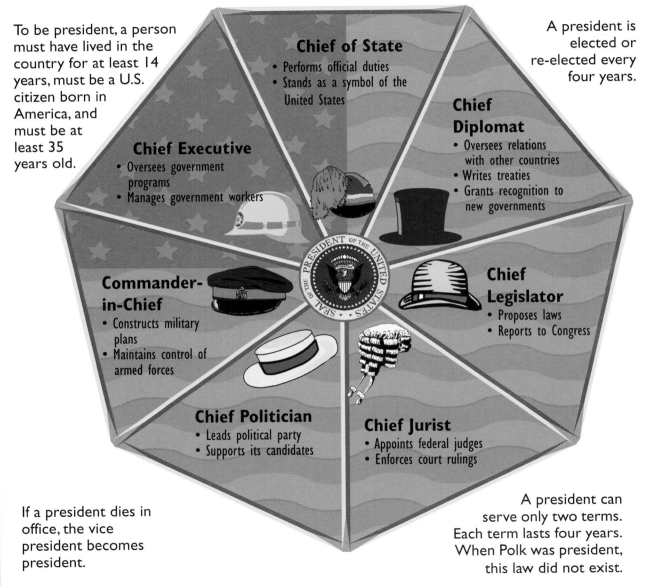

To be president, a person must have lived in the country for at least 14 years, must be a U.S. citizen born in America, and must be at least 35 years old.

A president is elected or re-elected every four years.

Chief of State
- Performs official duties
- Stands as a symbol of the United States

Chief Diplomat
- Oversees relations with other countries
- Writes treaties
- Grants recognition to new governments

Chief Executive
- Oversees government programs
- Manages government workers

Commander-in-Chief
- Constructs military plans
- Maintains control of armed forces

Chief Legislator
- Proposes laws
- Reports to Congress

Chief Politician
- Leads political party
- Supports its candidates

Chief Jurist
- Appoints federal judges
- Enforces court rulings

If a president dies in office, the vice president becomes president.

A president can serve only two terms. Each term lasts four years. When Polk was president, this law did not exist.

As president, James K. Polk had seven jobs.

The Three Branches of the U.S. Government

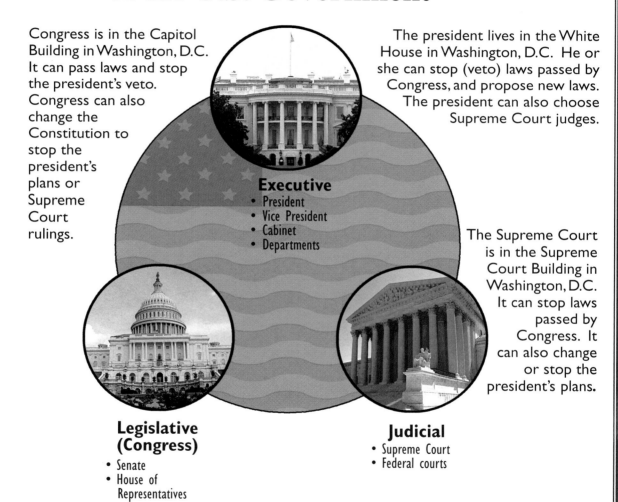

Congress is in the Capitol Building in Washington, D.C. It can pass laws and stop the president's veto. Congress can also change the Constitution to stop the president's plans or Supreme Court rulings.

The president lives in the White House in Washington, D.C. He or she can stop (veto) laws passed by Congress, and propose new laws. The president can also choose Supreme Court judges.

Executive
- President
- Vice President
- Cabinet
- Departments

The Supreme Court is in the Supreme Court Building in Washington, D.C. It can stop laws passed by Congress. It can also change or stop the president's plans.

Legislative (Congress)
- Senate
- House of Representatives

Judicial
- Supreme Court
- Federal courts

The U.S. Constitution formed three government branches. Each branch has power over the others. So no single group or person can control the country. The Constitution calls this "separation of powers."

President Polk

As president, Polk had four goals. He wanted to make a new U.S. **treasury** and lower taxes. He also wanted to establish a border between Oregon and Canada. And he wanted to make Texas and California part of the U.S.

In 1846, **Congress** passed the Independent Treasury Act. And it voted to lower taxes. Polk had reached two of his goals.

In 1818, England and the U.S. agreed in a **treaty** to share Oregon Territory. The treaty was renewed in 1827. Either country could end the treaty with a 12-month notice.

In 1846, Polk notified England that the U.S. was ending the treaty. He wanted the entire territory for the U.S. But England did not want to give it up.

Most Americans wanted the border just north of the fifty-fourth **parallel**, as Polk promised during his campaign.

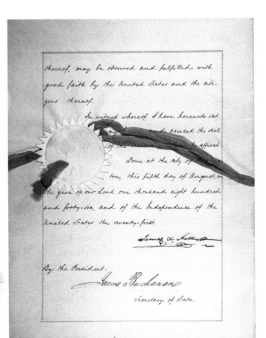

Secretary of State James Buchanan's signature on the Oregon Treaty

England wanted the border to be the Columbia River.

England and the U.S. had to **compromise**. In the Oregon **Treaty**, they agreed that Oregon's border would be along the forty-ninth **parallel**. Many people were upset at Polk's compromise. But he had settled the border question peacefully.

☐ **Oregon Territory**

54° 40' parallel

49° parallel

Columbia River

In 1844, President John Tyler had signed a document to **annex** Texas. Polk wanted to move ahead on the annexation. But Mexico still wanted to control Texas.

In 1845, Polk sent John Slidell to Mexico to settle the issue and to buy California. But Mexican officials would not meet with him.

Mexico believed Texas's southern boundary was the Nueces River. Polk believed its boundary was the Rio Grande. In 1846, Polk sent U.S. troops to the Rio Grande to protect Texas from the Mexicans.

Mexico considered this an **invasion**. Then on April 25, 1846, a group of Mexican soldiers fought with 63 American scouts. Sixteen scouts were killed. The Mexicans forced the others to **surrender**.

Mexican and American troops were soon fighting north of the Rio Grande. On May 13, 1846, **Congress declared** war on Mexico.

President John Tyler

22

In most battles, the Mexican army outnumbered American troops two to one. But the Americans had strong leaders such as Zachary Taylor and Ulysses S. Grant. They were also better organized. And Americans had guns and cannons that Mexico did not.

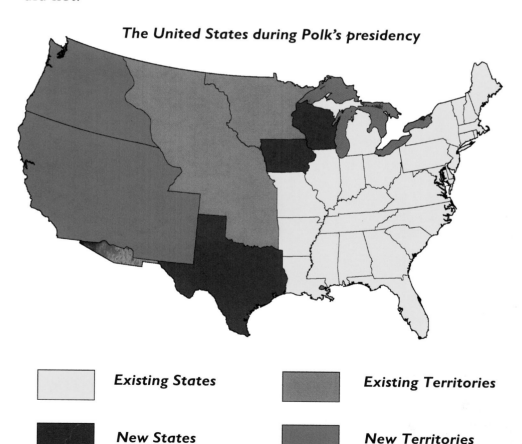

The United States during Polk's presidency

Existing States

Existing Territories

New States

New Territories

In 1848, the U.S. won the war. Polk wrote a **treaty** called the Treaty of Guadalupe Hidalgo. In it, the U.S. gave Mexico $15 million for Texas south to the Rio Grande. The U.S. also got California, Nevada, Utah, and parts of six other states.

Polk sent Nicholas Trist to **deliver** the treaty. The U.S. and Mexico signed it in 1848. The Mexican War was over. President Polk had reached all of his goals.

At the end of his term, Polk refused to be **nominated** for president again. He was tired. He wanted to go home and rest.

The Treaty of Guadalupe Hidalgo

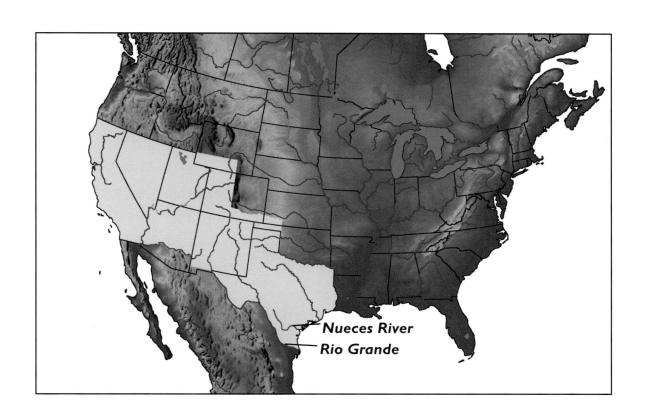

Nueces River

Rio Grande

Territory added to the U.S. by the Treaty of Guadalupe Hidalgo

Home to Polk Place

*I*n 1849, Polk left the White House. He and his wife Sarah bought Felix Grundy's old house in Nashville, Tennessee. They named it Polk Place.

The Polks took a steamboat back to Tennessee. But Polk became sick on the trip. He relaxed for a few months in his new home, but he never got better.

On June 15, 1849, Polk died. He was 54 years old. Sarah lived until 1891. She never remarried. The Polks were buried in the garden at Polk Place.

James K. Polk was one of America's most important **political** leaders. He **expanded** the country from coast to coast. He improved the economy. And he worked hard to support the **Democratic** party.

A rare photograph of James K. Polk

Fast Facts

- In 1848, James K. Polk announced that gold was found in California. His announcement started the California gold rush.

- Sarah Childress Polk had the song "Hail to the Chief" written for her husband. He was short, and afraid that no one would notice when he walked into a room. Now, at big events, the president's entrance is usually announced by this song.

- Henry Clay's campaign **slogan** in 1844 was "Who is James K. Polk?"

- The first annual White House Thanksgiving Dinner was hosted by Sarah Childress Polk.

- People called President Jackson Old Hickory because he was so tough. Polk helped President Jackson so much, people called him Young Hickory.

• In 1893, James and Sarah Polk's graves were moved from the garden at Polk Place to the state capital grounds in Nashville, Tennessee.

President Polk's grave

Glossary

annex - to add land to a nation.

bar exam - the test that a person must pass in order to become a lawyer.

committee - a group of people chosen to do one special task. The Committee on Ways and Means is a group of people working to raise money for the government.

compromise - settling an argument by having both sides give up some of what they want.

Congress - the lawmaking body of the U.S. It is made up of the Senate and the House of Representatives.

convention - a large meeting held for a special purpose.

dark horse - in horse racing, a dark horse is a horse that no one expects to win. In politics, a dark horse is the candidate who no one expects to win.

debt - something owed to someone, usually money.

debate - to discuss a question or topic.

declare - to make a formal public announcement.

deliver - to carry and give out.

Democrat - a political party. When Polk was president, Democrats supported farmers and landowners.

electoral college - the group that elects the president and vice president by casting electoral votes. When people vote for president, the political party that gets the most votes in each state sends its representatives to the electoral college. There they vote for their party's candidate.

eliminate - to get rid of or remove.

expand - to make bigger.

House of Representatives - a group of people elected by citizens to represent them. It meets in Washington, D.C., and makes laws for the nation. Most states also have a House of Representatives to make state laws.

invasion - to enter a country as an enemy and attack it.

investigation - a careful search.

lawyer - a person who knows the laws and acts for another person in a court of law.

nominate - to name a candidate for an office.

opponent - a person who takes the opposite position in a contest.

parallel - an imaginary line around the earth that marks degrees of latitude.
politics - the process of making laws and running a government.
secretary of state - a member of the president's cabinet who helps decide
    economic matters.
senate - a governing or lawmaking assembly.
slogan - a word or phrase used to express a position, a stand, or a goal.
Speaker of the House - the leader of the majority party in the House of
    Representatives who runs House sessions.
surplus - an amount over what is needed.
surrender - to give up.
treasury - a place where money is kept.
treaty - a formal agreement between two countries.
tutor - to be taught by a private teacher. The teacher is also called a tutor.
unite - to join together.
urethra - the tube that drains urine from the body.
Whig - a political party that was strong in the early 1800s but had ended by the
    1850s. The Whigs supported laws that helped business.

Internet Sites

The Presidents of the United States of America
http://www.whitehouse.gov/WH/glimpse/presidents.html
This site is from the White House.

PBS American Presidents Series
http://www.americanpresidents.org
This site from PBS has links and information about James K. Polk's life.

James K. Polk Ancestral Home
http://www.jameskpolk.com
This site tours James Polk's first home in Columbia, Tennessee.

These sites are subject to change. Go to your favorite search engine and type in
United States Presidents for more sites.

Index

jB
POLK

Welsbacher, Anne.

James K. Polk.

$21.35